Walt Disney's Comics and Stories
No. 663, December 2005
Published monthly by Gemstone Publishing,
© 2005 Disney Enterprises, Inc., except where noted.

ISBN 1-888472-03-0

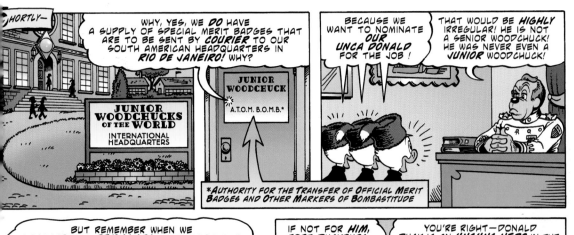

SHORTLY—

WHY, YES, WE *DO* HAVE A SUPPLY OF SPECIAL MERIT BADGES THAT ARE TO BE SENT BY *COURIER* TO OUR SOUTH AMERICAN HEADQUARTERS IN *RIO DE JANEIRO!* WHY?

JUNIOR WOODCHUCKS OF THE WORLD
INTERNATIONAL HEADQUARTERS

JUNIOR WOODCHUCK
A.T.O.M. B.O.M.B.*

BECAUSE WE WANT TO NOMINATE *OUR UNCA DONALD* FOR THE JOB!

THAT WOULD BE *HIGHLY IRREGULAR!* HE IS NOT A SENIOR WOODCHUCK! HE WAS NEVER EVEN A *JUNIOR* WOODCHUCK!

*AUTHORITY FOR THE TRANSFER OF OFFICIAL MERIT BADGES AND OTHER MARKERS OF BOMBASTITUDE

BUT REMEMBER WHEN WE LOCATED THE *REMNANTS* OF HISTORIC OLD *FORT DUCKBURG*? IT WAS *UNCA DONALD* WHO RESCUED THE LOGS FROM BEING GROUND TO PULP IN A MILL!?

IF NOT FOR *HIM*, FORT DUCKBURG COULD NOT HAVE BEEN *REBUILT* AS AN INTERNATIONAL SHRINE!

YOU'RE RIGHT—DONALD DUCK IS AN *UNSUNG HERO* IN THE ANNALS OF WOODCHUCKERY!

YES! WE WOULD BE *PROUD* TO ALLOW YOUR UNCLE TO MAKE THAT TRIP TO RIO FOR THE WOODCHUCKS!

WITH AN *OPEN-ENDED* PLANE TICKET SO HE COULD *STAY* IN BRAZIL FOR A WHILE?

YOU DRIVE A HARD BARGAIN! *AGREED!*

AND WITH JUNIOR WOODCHUCK *INFORMATION* ABOUT BRAZIL?

GASP! YOU GO *TOO FAR!* THE GUIDEBOOK IS FOR THE EYES OF WOODCHUCKS *ONLY!*

THE VERY IDEA!

MY GORGE *RISES* AT THE THOUGHT!

JUST A *CONDENSED* VERSION OF THE *BRAZIL* CHAPTER?

ONLY A *PAMPHLET!*

REMEMBEERRRR...

OH, VERY WELL! YOU WIN! *DONE!*

WOW! MERIT BADGES FOR "GUILT-INDUCING" "WHEEDLING AND PERSUADING"!

NO TIME TO SHOW OFF NOW— WE HAVE *WORK* TO DO!

RIGHT! WE NEED TO SEND OFF *TWO* TELEGRAMS!

ONE TO A CERTAIN PARTY IN *RIO*...

...AND THE OTHER TO SOMEONE IN *CHIHUAHUA!*

RIO DE JANEIRO, BRAZIL!

THIS IS SUPPOSED TO BE THE *MOST BEAUTIFUL* CITY IN THE WORLD! I COULD SURE STAND A LITTLE OF THAT!

I DON'T KNOW *WHY* THE KIDS WERE SO *ANXIOUS* FOR ME TO TAKE THIS COURIER JOB! DO THEY *PREFER* TO STAY AT *GRANDMA'S* AND LIKE IT WHEN I'M GONE?

⇥SIGH!⇤ I GUESS THEY JUST WANTED TO *GET RID OF ME* FOR A WHILE, JUST LIKE EVERYONE ELSE DOES! OH, WELL...

HOW DOES GENERAL HUEY SAY WE CAN *RECOGNIZE* HIS UNCLE?

"WATCH FOR THE PASSENGER WHOSE LOWER LIP IS DRAGGING THE PAVEMENT!"

OI! I SEE HIM!

BOM DIA, SENHOR DUCK! WE ARE REPRESENTATIVES OF THE JUNIOR WOODCHUCKS OF BRAZIL— RIO, TROOP 1!

REALLY? I WOULD NEVER HAVE GUESSED!

DON'T I NEED TO DELIVER THIS PACKAGE TO YOUR LOCAL *HEADQUARTERS?*

NÃO! WE WILL TAKE IT FOR YOU!

BUT WE HAVE A *NEW* MISSION FOR YOU SENT BY THE *DUCKBURG COMMAND!*

"BE AT THE OBSERVATION DECK ATOP *SUGAR LOAF MOUNTAIN* AT NOON TODAY! MORE INSTRUCTIONS WILL FOLLOW!"

WHAT'S THIS ALL ABOUT?

NO TIME TO WASTE! TAKE THIS *BONDE* TO THE CABLE CAR STATION RIGHT AWAY! *RÁPIDO!*

WE WILL TAKE YOUR SUITCASE TO THE HOTEL!

1755

I GUESS I'D BETTER FOLLOW DIRECTIONS! I LOSE *ENOUGH* JOBS AS IT IS! GETTING *FIRED* BY A BUNCHA' CAMPFIRE KIDDIES WOULD BE THE *LAST STRAW*...

HORTLY—

ALL ABOARD!

IT'S ALMOST *NOON,* AND THE CABLE CAR IS GETTING READY TO *LEAVE* FOR THE SUMMIT!

TELEFERICO PÃO

I'D BETTER HURRY! THAT APPOINTMENT SOUNDED *URGENT!* IF I MISS IT, I'LL REALLY FEEL LIKE A HORSE'S--

BOOMF!

YOU HEARD ME! GET THAT SMELLY *HORSE* OUT OF HERE! IT'S BAD ENOUGH *YOU* WANT TO RIDE IN THIS CROWDED CAR WITH THAT STUPID *HAT!*

HOKAY, HOKAY, DON' MAKE THE *POOSH!* I MIGHT PUNCH YOUR *EARBALL!*

PANCHITO? *PANCHITO PISTOLES?* IS THAT *YOU?*

QUIÉN?

SON A' MY GUN! *DONAL' DUCK!* MY OLD AMIGO! COME TO MY ARMS! IT IS *MUY BUENO* TO SEE YOU AGAIN!

SLURP!

LO SIENTO, SEÑOR MARTINEZ! YOU MUST *STAY HERE!* IF YOU SEE ANY *SEÑORITAS,* TELL THEM PANCHITO WILL BE RIGHT BACK!

SNORT!

WHAT BRINGS YOU HERE FROM *MEXICO?*

I TELL YOU ON BOARD THE CABLEY CAR, DONAL'! *VÁMONOS!*

WOLVERINE™

DAYS OF FUTURE PAST

In a future world torn apart by hatred of all mutants, Wolverine™ is one of the few remaining X-Men™ able to continue the fight against the Sentinels™. Direct from the "Days of Future Past" ™ storyline, this latest Marvel Select release is in scale with past releases and features an unarticulated Kitty Pryde.

Designed and produced by Toy Biz for Diamond Select Toys and Collectibles.

Join the Radicals at www.diamondselecttoys.com

SCULPTED BY STEVE KIWUS   ONLY AVAILABLE IN SPECIALTY STORES DECEMBER 2005!

MICKEY MOUSE in THE SPIRIT OF CHRISTMAS

IT'S THE DAY BEFORE CHRISTMAS! MICKEY HAS BEEN BUSY HELPING DOC STATIC WITH HIS LATEST INVENTION -- THE DREAM BEAMER -- A 3D VIRTUAL REALITY GENERATOR FUELLED BY THE STUFF THAT DREAMS ARE MADE OF...

LUCKY WE REMEMBERED TO CHECK THE TIME! THE STORES HAD ALMOST CLOSED!

YEAH! THAT WOULD HAVE BEEN A STINKY CHRISTMAS! NO GIFTS, NO FOOD!

D 2004-084

I GET SO ABSORBED WHEN I WORK ON A NEW INVENTION! ESPECIALLY A *COMPLEX* ONE LIKE THE DREAM BEAMER!

IT *WASN'T* TOUGH TO LEARN TO PROGRAM IT, THOUGH! I HOPE OUR FRIENDS LIKE THE PROGRAM I MADE -- I'VE *ALWAYS* DREAMED ABOUT VISITING SANTA'S WORKSHOP!

I BET THEY WILL!

HEY! SOMEONE'S BROKEN IN!

OH NO! THE DREAM BEAMER!

WELL, LOOK WHO CRASHED THE PARTY!

23 CANS OF BELUGA CAVIAR LATER...

IT'S CHRISTMAS DAY! I HAVEN'T MISSED IT! THE SPIRITS HAVE DONE IT ALL IN ONE NIGHT! THEY CAN DO ANYTHING THEY LIKE! OF COURSE THEY CAN! OF *COURSE* THEY CAN!

PETE!

ZZZZZZZ!

WAKE UP, PETE!

HUH! WHAT? WHO?

WHO *ARE* YA? WHATCHA DOIN' IN *HERE*? YA WANNA GET A PUNCH IN THE NOSE!?

I'M THE *SPIRIT OF CHRISTMAS*--AND I'VE COME TO--

THAT'S CRAZY! WH-WHAT DO YOU WANT?

I WANT TO SHOW YOU THREE VISIONS THIS NIGHT!

THE JOURNEY TO ONE OF YOUR PAST CHRISTMASES BEGINS!

WHAT ARE YOU TALKING ABOUT...?

YARGH!

THIS IS THE PRESENT CHRISTMAS, PETE! DO YOU RECOGNIZE THE HOUSE ACROSS THE STREET?

YEAH! OF *COURSE* I ~~O~~! THAT'S WHERE THE %#@½*# MOUSE LIVES!

THREE YEARS I'VE SPENT ON THE DREAM BEAMER! NOW IT'S GONE! ⇾SOB!⇽

THERE, THERE, DOC! IT'LL TURN UP!

AW, QUIT YER GRIPIN'! IF THE EGGHEAD FEELS SORRY FER HIMSELF, HE CAN MAKE A NEW ONE!

IS THAT HOW YOU FEEL ABOUT IT?

SURE! IT AIN'T *MY* PROBLEM! IT'S HOW THE WORLD WORKS, SEE!

HMM! I DON'T GOT FRIENDS, 'CEPT CREEPS LIKE SWAGMAN!

BUT WHO *CARES*? WHEN I SELL DOC'S GIZMO, I'LL GET ENOUGH CASH TO *BUY* THE FRIENDS I NEED!

ARE YOU SURE ABOUT THAT?

WAS IT A DREAM?

THE FOLLOWING DAY -- CHRISTMAS EVE!

DECK THE HALLS WITH BOUGHS OF HOLLY! FA-LA-LA-LA-LA, LA-LA-LA-LA!

QUIET, NOW!

WHERE ARE YOU *GOING*, PETE?

I...UHH... WELL--

WON'T YOU COME IN AND *JOIN* US FOR SOME EGGNOG AND A SLICE OF TURKEY?

LATER...

WELL, THANKS! I *GUESS*!

ANY TIME, PETE!

HMM! I GOT A WEIRD, WARM FEELING INSIDE! MAYBE I'M SICK?

WELL, WHAT DO YOU KNOW! OL' PETE GOT A WHIFF OF THE *CHRISTMAS SPIRIT*!

AND IF I'M RIGHT--

THE *DREAM BEAMER*! BUT HOW...?

"I FOUND PETE'S SOOTY FOOTPRINTS BY THE LAB! THEN I FOLLOWED HIM BACK TO HIS HIDEOUT!"

WITH AN OLD SHEET AND A FLASHLIGHT, I TURNED INTO A SPIRIT! THE REST WAS A CINCH!"

"I JUST PROGRAMMED THREE CHRISTMAS VISIONS INTO THE DREAM BEAMER!"

WALT DISNEY'S ANDOLD WILD DUCK IN MIGHTIER THAN THE SWORD

> IN DAYS OF YORE ON FOLKESTONE COAST THERE LIVED A HERO OF MIGHT AND MIEN! HIS NAME WAS ANDOLD TEMERARY... *THE WILD DUCK OF WALSTAEN!*

AN' I SAY WE *RUN HIM THROUGH!*

THORFINN THE VILE'S VIKINGS ARE SAID TO BE A DAY'S HIKE AWAY...

...AND TEMERARY HAS NO *DEFENSE* READY! NO *ANTI-INVASION* TACTICS!

NO *INSURANCE!*

D 97379

> *B*UT FOLKE-STONE WILL BE SAVED IN A MANNER NONE YET EXPECT! IT ALL BEGINS WITH A MOST UNUSUAL DISCOVERY...

IT'S TIME I DECREED OUR BATTLE PLAN! I TIRE OF LOAFING AND YEARN TO FIGHT!

LITTLE BO! ≈SNORT!≈ PLANNING TO DEFEND US WITH *CHAR-COAL?*

NAY, COMMANDANT! I'M MAKING A PORTRAIT OF THE *MOST IMPORTANT PERSON I KNOW!*

IMPORTANT? MUST BE *ME!* CROWN MY CONK AND CALL ME ARTHUR!

BO, I'M *TOUCHED!* BUT MY *BEAK'S* NAY LONG AS YOU'VE MADE IT! I DON'T HAVE A *BEARD!* AND...

AND IT'S NOT *YOU* I'M DRAWING! IT'S *THORFINN THE VILE!*

FORSOOTH! THORFINN THE... ≈SPLUTTER!≈

AYE! 'TIS HE!

PRITHEE *EXPLAIN!*

MISTER ANDOLD WANTS AN *EXPLANATION?!* *MAYBE* MISTER ANDOLD SHOULDN'T HAVE *INSULTED* MY ART!

HE WOULDN'T TELL ME A THING! I'D GIVE A KINGDOM TO KNOW WHY HE WAS DRAWING THORFINN THE VILE!

WHAT HO! BRUTUS, AN EASEL, AND *ANOTHER* VIKING PORTRAIT!

IF I FLATTER HIS ARTISTRY, HE'LL GIVE ME THE LOWDOWN!

ANDOLD POURS IT ON!

...AND YOU DRAW WITH THE *FINESSE* OF YOUR FINEST MOMENTS IN BATTLE! BRILLIANCE SO PURE...

THANKS! GLAD YOU'RE AN ART LOVER!

BUT WHAT *SET* YOU TO YOUR WORK?

POSTERS I SAW IN THE VILLAGE! SOME KNAVE PUT THEM UP LAST NIGHT!

THE POSTERS OFFER A *PRIZE,* COMMANDANT! *10,000* PENNIES FOR THE BEST PORTRAIT OF THORFINN THE VILE...

...WITH THE WINNER'S PURSE COMPLIMENTS OF THORFINN *HIMSELF!*

AND JUST LIKE THAT, IT'S IN STYLE TO BECOME AN ARTIST! WHO KNEW?

I'M GOING TO THE VILLAGE FOR A GANDER AT THOSE *POSTERS!* KEEP AN EYE OUT FOR TROUBLE, SQUIRE!

T'WILL BE A PITTANCE, COMMANDANT!

ANDOLD FINDS FOLKESTONE A HIVE OF DIZZY EXCITEMENT!

STAP MY VITALS! *EVERYONE'S* AT AN EASEL!

≈DROOL!≈ 10,000 PENNIES!

THORFINN THE VILE IS THORFINN THE *GENEROUS!*

HE *LOVES* US!

HE MUST BE HOLDING THE CONTEST TO *WARM* FOLKESTONE TO HIS PRESENCE!

OUR FIRST VIKING *ALLY* IN TIME IM- MEMORIAL!

AYDIS IS AT HER CANVAS, TOO!

≈SNORT!≈ EVEN *YOU'RE* CONTAMINATED BY THIS MANIA!

I LOVE DRAWING, MY LIEGE! AND I NEED THE REWARD...

...TO HAVE MY HUT'S *ROOF* REPAIRED! IT LOOKS LIKE STONEHENGE AFTER A STORM!

BUT I WORK *UNEASILY!* I FEAR A SINISTER *PURPOSE* BEHIND THIS CONTEST!

I SUSPECT THE SAME! BUT I'LL SETTLE OUR SUSPICIONS WITH AN *EXPEDITION!*

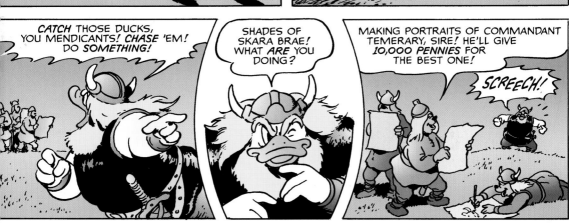

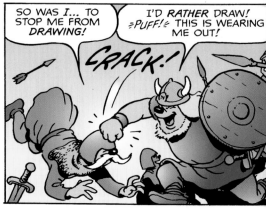

HAR! HAR! I *THOUGHT* SO! NOW I KNOW WHERE THEY *ARE!*

OOOPS!

NOT FAR AWAY!

NERTS! PRACTICAL ALWAYS MAKES US DO THESE *BORING CHORES!* LIKE GOING *SHOPPING* AT THE CRACK OF *DAWN!*

STOP WHINING! MY ARMLOAD IS HEAVIER!

ZIGGITY DIGGITY! RING THE BELL FOR *BRUNCH!*

⇥YIPES!⇤ THE WOLF!

HELP! HELP!

PRACTI-CAL!

THIS WAY, QUICK, BROTHERS! COME ON IN!

SAVED IN THE NICK OF TIME! NOW TO BLOCK THE DOOR!

⇥PUFF! PUFF!⇤

BONK!

⇥GASP! PUFF⇤ DADBLAST IT! I'VE GOTTA GET IN BETTER SHAPE!

BUT I AIN'T LOST *YET!* I'LL JUST HIDE BEHIND THIS TREE!

SOONER OR LATER THEY'LL *HAFTA* COME OUT TO RUN THEIR *ERRANDS,* AND THEN–*HEE! HEE!*

Walt Disney's **GOOFY** in *Miracle on Main Street*

GOOFY AND MICKEY PROUDLY MAKE THE MOST OF CHRISTMAS EVE BY MOONLIGHTING AT MERCENARY'S DEPARTMENT STORE—

YOU'RE NEXT TO SEE SANTA, LITTLE GIRL!

→HO-HO-HO!← COME ON UP HERE AN' TELL OL' SANTA YER *NAME*, MUH DEAR!

Santa's Christmas Consulting

D 99040

MY NAME'S REGINA! I LIVE AT 329 MAIN STREET!

→HO-HO!← AN' WHUT DO *YOU* WANT FER CHRISTMAS, REGINA?

THIS COMPANY MAKES DOLLS LOOK LIKE *ANY* LITTLE GIRL AT ALL! I WANT A DOLL THAT LOOKS EXACTLY LIKE *ME*!

ONLY $125

→GULP!← IS THET HER *PRICE* OR HER *SOCIAL SECURITY NUMBER*?!

WELL, REGINA, I'M NOT *SURE*—BUT I'LL *WORK* ON IT! →HO-HO-*HYUCK!*←

WORK ON IT?! YOU SURE DON'T *TALK* LIKE *SANTA!*

H-HE'S JUST GOT A LOT ON HIS *MIND*, IT BEING CHRISTMAS EVE!

BUT HE'S SANTA, ALL RIGHT! HE'S GOT SANTA'S LIST—*AND* THE SANTA *SPIRIT!*

BREAK TIME, "SANTA"! LET'S HIT THE LOCKER ROOM!

→HO-HO-*HO*-HUM!← THIS COSTUME'S LIKE AN *OVEN!* MUH *LEG'S* GONE TA SLEEP!

AND GOOFY'S CAUTION IS TAKING SOME TIME OFF, TOO—

THERE'S SOMETHING FISHY ABOUT THAT SANTA, AND I'M GONNA FIND OUT WHAT!

OOOOOH, *THAT'S* THUH SPOT!

GAWRSH, MICKEY, I LOVE THUH KIDS AN' ALL, BUT I'M NOT SHURE I'M *UP* TA THIS JOB! IT'S AN AWFUL *BIG* RESPONSIBILITY!

SCRATCH!

SCRATCH!

→GASP!← HE *IS* A FAKE!

A LITTLE TO THUH LEFT, MICKEY...

NOT UP TO YOUR JOB?! NIGHT-BEFORE-CHRISTMAS *NONSENSE,* GOOFY! YOU'RE A *GREAT* SANTA!

SCRATCH! SCRATCH!

YOU'RE A GREAT BIG *PHONY* IS WHAT YOU ARE! I KNEW IT! IT'S ALL A BIG *LIE!* →SOB!←

SANTA ISN'T REAL! I SAW HIM IN THE LOCKER ROOM! HE'S JUST A GUY IN A *COSTUME!*

I *KNEW* IT! *THERE IS NO* SANTA CLAUS!

UH, OH!

BACK SOON

WAAAAAH!

HOW *DARE* YOU LEAD OUR CHILDREN TO BELIEVE THERE'S NO SANTA?! LET'S GET *OUT* OF HERE!

WAIT! *PLEASE!*

YEAH! SIMMER DOWN— I MEAN, HO-HO-*HOLD ON* THERE! ALL *IS* WELL!

WAAAAAH!

OH, SO?

YOU'D BETTER DO SOMETHING TO WIN *BACK* THE FAITH OF THOSE KIDS, OR YOU'RE *FIRED!* UNDERSTAND?!

Y-YESSIR!

STORE OWNER

WE'VE *GOTTA* COME UP WITH A SOLUTION— AND *FAST!*

IF I GREW A REAL BEARD AND DRANK LOTSA *MILKSHAKES,* I'D LOOK MORE LIKE THUH REAL SANTA!

NO TIME FOR THAT— EVEN AT THE RATE *YOU* DRINK MILKSHAKES!

I KNOW! WE'LL GET *REGINA* THET *DOLL* THET LOOKS LIKE 'ER!

THAT'LL ONLY FIX *US* UP IN REGINA'S EYES! WE NEED TO RESTORE HER BELIEF IN *SANTA*...AND IN *YOUR* SANTA SPIRIT!

↓EXIT↓

IT'S LIKE I WAS TELLING HER BEFORE...

WOW! I'VE GOT IT! GOOFY, WE'RE GONNA TAKE YOUR PLAN *ONE STEP FARTHER!*

HUH?!

WHATEVER YOU'RE UP TO HAD BETTER *WORK*—OR I'LL HAVE YOU *ARRESTED* FOR *CORRUPTING MINORS!*

STEP TWO— REINDEER!

I SUBBED AS AN ASSISTANT ZOOKEEPER A COUPLE YEARS AGO! I HOPE THEY REMEMBER ME *FONDLY* ENOUGH TO DO US A *FAVOR*!

ZOO

ZOOKEEPER

...SO YOU SEE, "SANTA'S" GOTTA HAVE *REINDEER* TO CONVINCE REGINA WE'RE THE REAL DEAL!

QUITE A STORY, MICKEY! *I'VE A* GRANDDAUGHTER THAT AGE—BIT OF A SKEPTIC HERSELF!

BUT IF THUH KIDS *LOSE FAITH*, IT'LL *ALL BE MY FAULT*!

NOW, NOW! NEVER SAID I WOULDN'T HELP! I'LL LOAN YOU THE DEER, AND THEY'RE *TAME* ENOUGH TO WALK ON *LEASHES*!

BUT BOYS, I'VE ONLY GOT *SIX*! SEEMS TO ME SANTA USES *EIGHT*!

⸬UH-OH!⸬ IT'S NOT A *COMPLETE SET*, MICKEY!

NO, BUT SIX REINDEER ARE—⸬GULP!⸬ BETTER THAN NONE!

⸬FWEET!⸬ LET'S GO, REINDEER! DON'T I COMMAND ANY *AUTHORITY*?

⸬ARGH!⸬ IF IT'S *THIS* HARD TO PLAY SANTA, MAYBE WE OUGHT TO *GIVE UP*...

BUT MOUSETON *NEEDS* US—AND ITS *KIDS* NEED OUR SANTA *SPIRIT*! THEY'VE GOTTA BELIEVE!...RIGHT?!

AND HOW ELSE COULD WE GET YOU THE *DOLL* YOU ASKED FOR?

⇒SIGH!⇐ YOU GUYS AREN'T SO BAD! AND I APPRECIATE ALL THE TROUBLE YOU WENT TO, JUST TO PROVE TO ME THERE'S A SANTA!

BUT I GUESS I'M OLD ENOUGH NOW TO ACCEPT THAT HE JUST ISN'T REAL!

SAY IT AIN'T SO, REGINA! O' *COURSE* THERE'S A SANTA! I'M ONLY SORRY HE MAY SEE ME *STUCK* HERE!

THERE MUST BE *SOME* WAY TO CONVINCE YOU!

SORRY—BUT THANKS FOR TRYING, GUYS! I'M GETTING COLD, AND I SHOULD GO BACK TO BED!

Ching-Ching-Ching-Ching!

SLEIGH BELLS!... *SANTA CLAUS!*

⇒HO-HO-HO!⇐ *HERE'S* A SIGHT I DON'T SEE EVERY CHRISTMAS!

THANKS, SANTA!

THANK *YOU*, GOOFY! WHILE IT'S REALLY *MY* JOB TO KEEP CHILDREN BELIEVING IN ME...

...I ALSO OWE IT TO *OTHERS* SPREADING MY *SPIRIT* OF YULETIDE WARMTH! THAT SPIRIT *LIVES* IN PEOPLE LIKE GOOFY!

JUST BETWEEN US, REGINA, I *ALSO* LIKE LOCKER ROOM BREAKS!

OH, *THANK* YOU, SANTA! NOW I HAVE *TWO* VERY SPECIAL DOLLS!

REGINA SURE IS HAPPY!

SAY, IF SANTA'S EVEN BIGGER THAN *I* AM, HOW DOES *HE* GET DOWN THUH CHIMNEY?

I WOULDN'T WORRY ABOUT IT, GOOFY! I'M SURE ST. NICK HAS IT ALL FIGURED OUT!

WALT DISNEY
PRESENTS
CHIP 'N DALE

W WDC 89-16

W WDC 89-16

ONE WINTER, DONALD GAILY GOES UP IN THE HILLS AFTER IT SNOWS! HE RENTS A CABIN! **BRR!** ALL NIGHT HE SHIVERS, WAITING FOR DAYLIGHT!

HE LOOKS FOR WOOD TO BUILD A FIRE! THE EMPTY WOOD BOX ROUSES IRE!

HE GRABS THE AXE! "THEY CAN'T FREEZE ME," HE SAYS, "I'LL GO CHOP DOWN A TREE!"

HE SEES A TREE STUMP! IT LOOKS GOOD! "AHA!" HE SAYS, "THAT'S **EASY** WOOD!"

THOUGH DONALD DUCK IS UNAWARE, TWO CHIPMUNKS, CHIP AND DALE, LIVE THERE! THE KNOTHOLE IS THEIR LITTLE DOOR! THEIR NUTS ARE PILED HIGH ON THE FLOOR!

WHAM! WHACK! AS DONALD CHOPS THE TREE, THEY'RE SHAKEN UP CONSIDERABLY!

THEY FALL OUT THROUGH THE KNOTHOLE WHEN THE DUCK PICKS UP THE LOG... AND THEN ...

ONE WAITS UNTIL THE OTHER SCAMPERS UP THE HILL!

DALE STARTS A SNOWBALL, FOR HE KNOWS IT WILL GROW BIGGER AS IT GOES!

AND CHIP KNOCKS LOUDLY ON THE DOOR! HE POUNDS UNTIL HIS PAWS ARE SORE!

TO DONALD IT'S A TAPPING SOUND! HE'S STARTLED AND HE LOOKS AROUND!

HE OPENS UP THE DOOR .. AND **SMASH** THE SNOWBALL COMES IN WITH A **CRASH**!

WHILE DONALD SPUTTERS IN THE SNOW, THE CHIPMUNKS TAKE THEIR LOG... AND GO!

KJD002-1

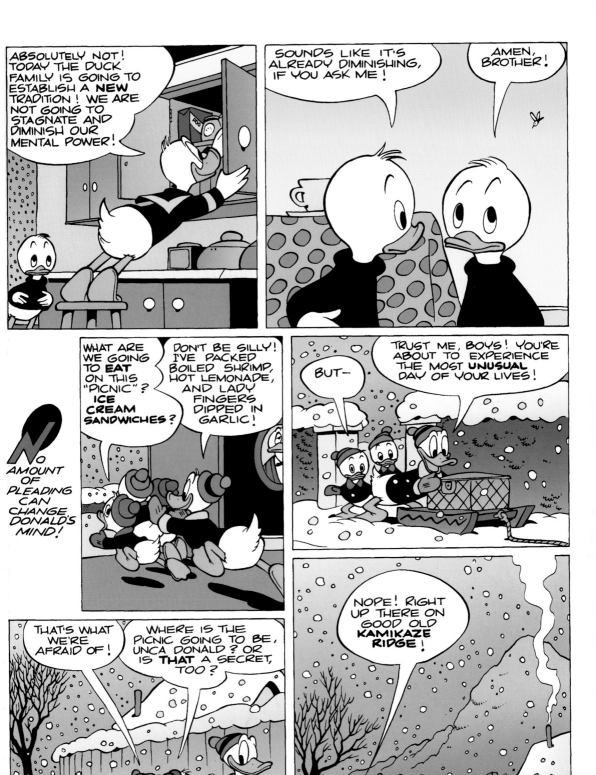

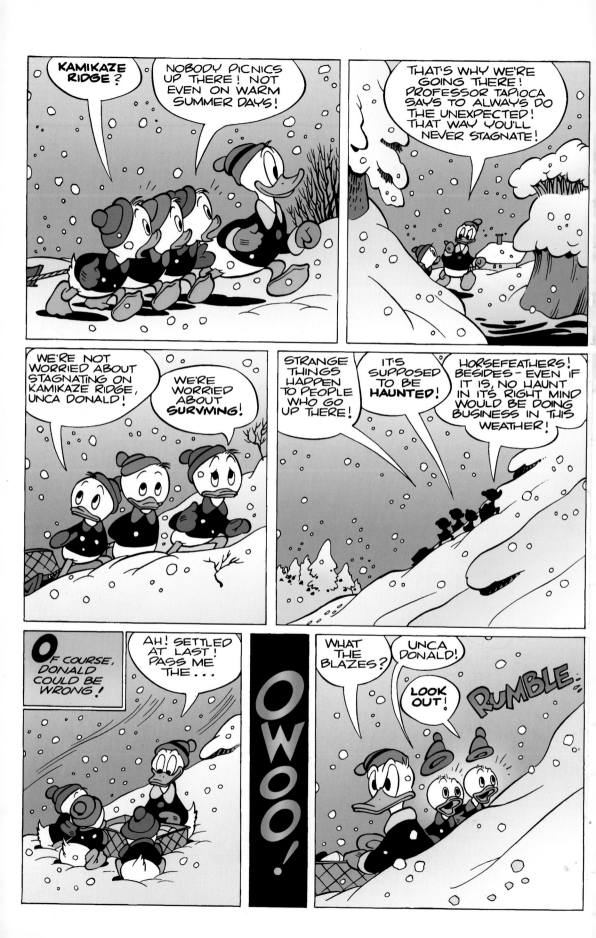

RANT! RAVE!

WE COULDN'T GET AROUND THE ROCKS, UNCA DONALD! WHAT'S ALL THE YELLING ABOUT?

I'VE BEEN ATTACKED **TWICE** BY THAT SIMPLE-MINDED OLD TREE TRUNK OVER THERE!

WHAT OLD TREE TRUNK?

WAK! IT'S **GONE!**

OLD TREE TRUNKS DON'T WALK AROUND IN THE SNOW!

AND EVEN IF THEY DID—THEY WOULDN'T LEAVE SIZE **16** BOOT TRACKS! LOOK!

SOMEONE UP HERE IS TRYING TO **SPOIL** OUR PICNIC!

OH, RIGHT!

BUT **WHO?** AND **WHY?**

WHO CARES! I VOTE WE GO HOME AND ENJOY WHAT'S LEFT OF THE DAY!

YEAH! WE HAVEN'T EVEN **EATEN** YET!

BUT DONALD IS DETERMINED TO FOLLOW THE TRACKS TO THEIR SOURCE AND WREAK HIS VENGENCE...

THIS GUY MUST BE HALF MOUNTAIN GOAT!

YEAH, AND WE MUST BE HALF **NUTS**!

FINALLY...

AN OLD SHACK!

DO YOU SEE WHAT I SEE?

AND THE TRACKS LEAD RIGHT TO IT!

OUR FROLICSOME FRIEND SEEMS TO HAVE GOTTEN AWFULLY CARELESS ALL OF A SUDDEN!

HE PROBABLY FIGURED NOBODY WOULD BE DETERMINED ENOUGH TO FOLLOW HIM THIS FAR!

OKAY! ON THE COUNT OF THREE, WE'LL CRASH THE JOINT! READY? ONE... TWO...

...THREE!

CRASH

THE PLACE IS EMPTY!

OH, NO IT ISN'T! YAK! YAK! YAK! IT'S FULL OF MEDDLESOME DUCKS WHO ARE ABOUT TO GO FOR A LITTLE **RIDE**!

CRASH

KARUMF

WELL WELL! AREN'T WE THE COZY LOT!

GET YOUR HAIR OUT OF MY MOUTH!

THAT'S MY HEAD YOU'RE SITTING ON!

GRUMF!

THE TANGLE IS SOON UNTANGLED . . .

HANK THE HERMIT! SO YOU'RE THE REASON PEOPLE THOUGHT THAT KAMIKAZE RIDGE WAS HAUNTED!

YEP! I HATE PEOPLE! IT WAS A GOOD WAY TO KEEP 'EM OUT OF MY HAIR!

I USED ALL KINDS OF NEAT TRICKS TO SCARE 'EM OFF! SNOWBALLS, TRAPS, DISGUISES, AND EVEN VENTRILOQUISM!

AHA! THAT EXPLAINS THE TALKING SNOWBALL!